# BELINDA GOODRICH

# Kick-Ass
# PROJECT
# MANAGER

## THE HANDBOOK FOR PROJECT
## MANAGEMENT SUCCESS

# Kick-Ass Project Manager

*The Handbook for Project Management Success*

Belinda Goodrich

BelindaGoodrich.com
PMLearningSolutions.com

GOODRICH PUBLISHING
Phoenix, Arizona

www.BelindaGoodrich.com     |     www.GoodrichPublishing.com

Ordering Information:

Special discounts are available on quantity purchases by corporations, associations, educators, and others. For details, contact the publisher at the above listed address.

*To my Dad…*

*You always encouraged me to work hard and get shit done.*
*So I'm doing it!*


*Miss you every hour of every day. Thank you for raising me*
*to be a strong and fierce power player.*

*Don Goodrich 11/28/1936 – 11/05/2017*


*#SolaGratia*

*#2018Strong*

# CONTENTS

# Introduction

I like to say that I was born a project manager. Not by choice, but simply through life events. Thankfully I've always been pretty good at it. I love the satisfaction of taking something nebulous, establishing an approach and a structure, and delivering a tangible end-product. The more difficult and the messier the project, the more I like it.

Having said that, as a child I didn't dream of one day being a project manager. (Does any excited school-age kid ever say, "I want to be a project manager when I grow up!"?).

I certainly didn't. I wanted to be a forensic pathologist (thanks to my first crush, Jack Klugman, as Quincy). Looking back at it now, I can see the correlations between investigating a medical case and project management (or am I just really reaching here?).

The reality was that my parents owned a business and in that day and age, it was a roll-up-your-sleeves, all hands on-deck approach to business operations. I could say I officially started "working" at age nine. When I say working, I mean being paid for doing activities. After school and on vacation weeks, I was at my parent's child care facility. Not as a kid, but as a staff member. I also spent most weekends babysitting for an established set of clients.

I would develop pre-school art projects, cutting out the shapes, gathering the supplies, ensuring that all the materials were ready. I cleaned, cleaned, and cleaned some more. I let the parents know how their kiddos did during the day. I was nine going on 30.

My first big project came when I was 16. My parent's child care center offered care for children two and a half and up. Based on customer requests, my mother decided to investigate offering infant and toddler care. She asked me to do the research on the licensing requirements, equipment needs, pricing, and anything else involved in creating this new offering. Using the well-worn book published by the state, I carefully measured our available space and the price point for a suitable return on investment. It looked to be a worthwhile investment.

I designed the space, ordered the equipment, and interviewed infant and toddler caregivers. While I cannot say for certain what the candidates were thinking, I would guess they were surprised that they were being interviewed by a teenager. With an updated license, we opened our availability to infants and toddlers and added a crucial component to the business. Project number one was a success.

And I was hooked.

After college and after relocating to Arizona in the 1990s, I was hired for my first official project management position. I challenged the status quo, caused a little bit of trouble, saved my employers a lot of money, and got a lot of great stuff done. I quickly moved up the ranks and eventually landed a coveted job as a Director of project management. One day, I realized I wanted more than the office, more than the title, more than the salary. I wanted to instill a passion for project management in organizations.

Fast forward to 2018 and I love being a consultant, speaker, coach, and trainer related to all topics project management. Project managers can be the life-blood of an organization. And if they are not, then management needs to take a long, hard look at how they intend to achieve their strategic goals. Multiple professional project management designations and credentials exist, and skilled and experienced project managers demand a high salary. It is a good time to be a project manager!

Unfortunately, most project managers that I work with are coming out of one of three stables:

- Intuitive project managers who just have a natural proclivity to organize complex activities
- Trained project managers who have learned (sometimes rigid and process-heavy) methodologies and approaches to achieving project objectives
- Technical experts that assume the role of a project manager when a change to their technical realm is needed

We know that effective project management is critical to an organization's success. And you know that your ability to be a successful project manager directly impacts your career trajectory and salary. So how do you go from being an ok or intuitive project manager to being a kick-ass project manager?

That is where this book comes into play. I have captured years of lessons learned not only from my individual experiences but also from hundreds of my peers, students, mentees, and other project management trainers. Using that feedback, I have identified nine topics to aid you in improving and mastering your project management effectiveness.

What you will *not* find in this book, however, are the traditional and fundamental aspects of being a project manager: running a kick-off meeting, creating a schedule, building a Gantt chart, or developing a risk register. I give you way more credit than that and know that if you are reading this book, you already know that stuff. This book escalates you and your performance above the basics!

# Chapter 1

# Know Yourself

I am going to just jump right into the tough stuff. Without this first chapter, the rest of the chapters are not really worth very much. This is your honesty inventory. While, generally speaking, people tend to be their own biggest critic, it is interesting how difficult it is for most people to do an accurate assessment of their flaws, especially as it relates to their business and work skills and techniques.

I believe this is due in part to our need to protectively establish ourselves as a valuable contributor within the corporate hierarchy. But let's get real, folks, there is always something we can do to improve. It is time for you to be honest with yourself.

## Step One: Acknowledge That You Can Improve

Make the acknowledgement: I can make improvements in my project management skills, capabilities, techniques, and approaches.

The first step is admitting that we have a problem, right?

Project managers that are resistant to change and self-growth tend to limit themselves from a career-perspective and end up burnt out and resentful. This is not enjoyable for you, or the people around you, including your family, friends, and co-workers.

Our view of ourselves is distorted, typically leading to an inaccurate assessment of our strengths and weaknesses. The thing we may perceive as our greatest strength may be seen as our biggest weakness by others.

I have always been an aggressive, go-getter. I get STUFF done. I see this as my best attribute. What company wouldn't value the project manager that understands the project objective and goes full steam ahead towards obtaining that objective?

8

What I came to realize, however, was that my greatest strength was also a great weakness. My team members and peers perceived me as setting difficult, if not impossible standards. Despite the fact that I verbally reinforced the contrary, they read my behavior as an expectation of their behavior. I worked 70 hours per week, so I must expect them to work 70 hours per week.

When it came to problem-solving, I was like a dog with a bone, relentless until a solution was identified. They took that as it is not acceptable to ask for help; if they were, in fact, capable then they should be able to solve the problem themselves. Needless to say, this was not my belief at all.

## Step Two: Create Your Assessment

Begin with identifying what you believe to be your top five strengths and your top five weaknesses. To assist, think about the role of a project manager with these questions:

- How mature is my project management practice?
- How strong is my technical project management expertise?
- How does my team perceive me? Leader? Task manager? Unwilling accomplice? Peer?

- How do my stakeholders perceive me? My sponsor? My peers?
- How is my communication? Written? Verbal?
- Am I consistent with my project information and status communication?
- Do I keep my project documentation up-to-date?
- Do I actively seek creative solutions to problems?
- Would I be perceived as an optimist? Pessimist? Realist?
- Do I convey and inspire confidence? Or hesitancy?
- What one word would people use to describe me?
- What are the gaps in my project management approach?
- What is the one area where I need the most improvement?
- How well do I listen? Do I listen with the intent to respond or to understand?
- Do I "roll up my sleeves" and get the work done?
- How do I treat my team members?
- Do I impact my team members work environment? For better or for worse?
- Would I prefer an open / shared work environment or a private cube or office?

- What does my every day demeanor say about me? Stressed? Happy? Excited? Frustrated?
- Do I "gossip" with my team or peers?
- What expectations do I place on my team members?
- How often do I seek out opportunities for growth and improvement?
- I am considered the "go-to" person for _____ ?
- How do I make the people around me feel?

Once you have identified some key areas, create a survey to collect feedback. I recommend keeping the survey/assessment somewhat simple, yet informative. If it is too long, it will be difficult to secure enough responses to be valuable. A numerical scale of one to nine, or something similar will yield the most telling results. Include open-ended questions, as well.

## Step Three: Identify Your Assessors

It is imperative that we actively solicit and embrace feedback from those around us. This isn't always an easy thing to do – who wants to hear about their flaws? But it is a critical element to self-growth and development. Asking your best buddy at work to assess you may not result in an actionable list.

Go to those that you have experienced challenges with in the past – essentially talk to the people that don't appear to like you. They will typically be the most honest.

Create a broad sampling pool to account for non-responders. It is important that different roles, titles, and relationships are explored. Consider interactions you have had in the past and potentially people you will be interacting with in the future that may have knowledge of you.

## Step Four: Seek Feedback From Your Assessors

Most people are uncomfortable with providing honest feedback to someone – especially someone they care about or must work with on a regular basis. To combat this, the set-up to asking for and receiving the feedback must come from a sincere desire to actually listen, act, and change.

In this day and age of electronic communication, I strongly recommend actually having an in-person or over-the-phone conversation with the assessors. This gives you an opportunity to convey your desire for honest feedback and should also include a discussion on how you intend to act upon the information.

Convey to your assessors:

- What you are asking them to do

- Why you are asking them to do it
- How you will be collecting their feedback
- When you will be requesting it and when you need it completed
- What they can expect as a follow-up and/or outcome

Be sure to express your need for honest feedback and your appreciation of their input. Set a deadline for returning the feedback.

## Step Five: Analyze the Feedback

And now it's time to see how others perceive you. While it can be a little unsettling and even discouraging, remember the intent of the exercise is to make you better and stronger as a project manager. While challenging, it is imperative that you set aside the emotional response and focus on the practical aspect of evaluating the feedback.

It is perfectly acceptable to "put aside" any outlying scores when calculating your "scores", however, do not discard them. They are valuable, as well.

I had asked a number of my peers and stakeholders to assess me on a number of factors. On a scale of $1 - 9$, I received all 8s and 9s on my communication effectiveness, with the exception from one particular stakeholder. This stakeholder,

Mary, and I had a colorful history marked by a lot of disagreement. My first reaction to seeing her low score was "oh that figures", however, I had to do some introspection – was my communication with Mary ineffective? Why? Was it due to seeds of bitterness I had been holding on to?

I reviewed some of my recent emails with her and found that I truly was very quick and relatively unfriendly on my responses. I did not elaborate on topics of discussion and re-reading the emails made me realize that they certainly could come across as dismissive. I reached out to Mary and asked for a 1:1 to discuss her feedback.

She confirmed that she "picked up a tone" in my emails. She also explained that she has difficulty sometimes following me on conference calls because I talk quickly and moved through the agenda at a fast pace. This proved to be a very eye-opening discussion for me and one that really put Mary and I in a much better place moving forward. She appreciated my effort to understand her feedback and work on improvements.

Your weaknesses will be illuminated through this feedback process and it's critical to find out why you have that behavior or weakness - working on the cause versus the effect. If you just say "oh, my communication sucks, I'll work on it" without realizing the "why" behind your sucky communication, you will not change. Look for the cause!

## Step Six: Identify Your Strengths and Weaknesses

Using the results from the survey or assessments, identify your strengths and weaknesses. Compare your results with your self-inventory. Identify those areas where there is a misalignment between your self-perception and the perception of others.

How do you move a mountain? One rock at a time. Do not attempt to fix all of your weaknesses at once (I trust you will have more than one. You are human, after all!) Pick the top one or two – not only from a score-perspective, but also from an impact-perspective.

It is helpful to apply the Pareto principle to this – 80% of the problems come from 20% of the causes – focus on that 20% in order to eliminate 80% of the problems. Resist the urge to feel like you need to fix it all immediately. It will come in time. It has taken you a lifetime to develop your habits and behaviors; it is not going to change overnight.

Remember to evaluate your strengths as well. Were you surprised by what your feedback revealed? As with your weaknesses, select the top one or two strengths that were revealed. How can you further develop those areas? Can you possibly help others in those areas? Learn to play up to your strengths and wear those strengths as a badge of honor.

## Step Seven: Establish Short-term and Long-term Goals and an Action Plan

I cannot emphasize enough the importance of this step. You have your data – now use it! And the best way to use it is to set goals. Many of the weak areas you will be addressing and the strong areas you will be growing, will take some work. Do not expect overnight and immediate change. Set small, incremental goals to be achieved in the short-term that will lead to the attainment of goals in the long-term.

First think about what your end-state looks like when you've achieved your goals. From there, start breaking the vision down into long-term goals. Break the long-term goals down into short-term goals. This reminds me of a line from the movie, *What About Bob*: "Baby steps, Bob, baby steps".

The most common framework for goal development is the SMART criteria:

- S – Specific or significant
- M – Measurable or meaningful
- A – Attainable or action-oriented

- R – Relevant or rewarding
- T – Time-bound or trackable

For example, instead of having "become a professional project manager" as a goal, it is more powerful to use the SMART goal "successfully complete my PMP credential by December 31, 2018."

Once you have your list of goals complete, prioritize them, and develop your action plan. Writing down your goals and having them somewhere to visually remind you of your intentions can help keep you focused.

## Step Eight: Update (and Thank) the Assessors

Your assessors took the time and energy to provide feedback. Be sure to confirm with them that you took the feedback seriously and what you intend to do with the information. Be sure to follow-up with any of those "outlier" scores or comments.

It is imperative that you do not come across as defensive, argumentative, or dismissive of their feedback. Keep in mind that you will want to reuse these resources in the future to measure your improvement in your behaviors and skills.

## Step Nine: Re-survey and Re-align

You may think you have improved and grown but would your assessors agree? Periodically re-survey your assessors. For those assessors that were particularly outspoken, detailed, and/or honest, schedule time with them to have a discussion regarding your progress.

## Additional Recommended Exercise: Stop | Start | Continue

I absolutely love this very powerful yet simple exercise. Ask your project team members:

1.  What are three things you would like me to stop doing?
2.  What are three things you would like me to start doing?
3.  What are three things you would like me to continue doing?

This is an incredibly revealing exercise with multiple benefits. The fact that you are asking for feedback demonstrates your commitment to the team and to your self-development, earning you leadership points. You will harvest valuable information about simple things that can make a big difference to your team: happy team, happy project, happy stakeholders. Your follow-up on these actions will inspire your team to trust you and recognize your commitment to them.

I had recently assumed responsibility for a team that had weathered some pretty difficult times and circumstances. They were frustrated, distrustful, and less than thrilled that I was coming in as their new manager. After a few months in my role, I did the stop/start/continue exercise with them. They chose to do it as a team and I was really impressed and surprised with the feedback:

**Stop:**

1. Staying in your office with the door closed in the morning
2. Multi-tasking during meetings
3. Staying late on Friday

**Start:**

1. Socializing with us a bit in the morning
2. Taking lunch breaks
3. Asking for help

**Continue:**

1. Learning about each of us, personally and professionally
2. Having our backs and being proud to be our leader

3. Being a creative problem solver with a great "can-do" attitude

What I learned from this exercise is that little things really do make a big difference, but that I cannot be the one to determine what those "things" are. It needs to come from team and those around me.

# Chapter 1 Action Plan

My key takeaways and "Ah-has!" from this chapter:

_____

_____

_____

Why these takeaways are important:

_____

_____

_____

Target dates for implementation:

_____

_____

_____

# Chapter 2

# Know Everyone Else

One of the fundamental tenets of customer service is to know your customers. This really comes in to play with project management. And it is not just your customer; it is anyone and everyone with whom you will be interacting with and engaging.

Consider yourself a change agent. As a change agent, you will be making waves throughout the organization, just as a pebble tossed in a pond makes ripples to the shore. Consider who those ripples will touch.

Keep your friends close, keep your enemies closer. This is especially true in project management. I want to know who can help me propel the pebble and I need to know who is going to serve as a breaker to my ripples.

In project management, our objective is surprisingly simple: deliver value on the project objectives. What or, more importantly, who may stand in my way? You could have the most awesome, incredible, happy, fun, and perfect project and yet there will always be someone that does not want it to be a success. Their reasons may be self-serving or more altruistic. Knowing their motivations for the resistance will allow you to better respond in a way that ideally minimizes the impact.

## Find the Playmaker

While keeping your enemies closer is a good rule, do not forget to identify and seek out those who can help further your cause. In my experience, there are always those in the organization who know how to "work the system" and simply just get things done and make things happen. Oftentimes that individual has an organizational power and influence that is not directly related to title. I call this person the Playmaker and every organization has at least one.

Working at a large financial services firm, it did not take me long to identify the Playmaker: a petite and unassuming team member named Shirley. Standing no more than 4'10", Shirley knew everyone, knew everything, and most importantly knew how to navigate the human and political landscape of the organization. I learned very quickly that being on Shirley's good side would provide me with deep insight into the company and the people.

One of my favorite movies is Shawshank Redemption. In that movie, the character Ellis Boy "Red" Redding, played by Morgan Freeman, is a Playmaker. When Andy Dufresne, the new prisoner to the yard, is told that Red is a man who can get things, he approaches Red with a request.

"I'm known to locate certain things from time to time" Red responds. And he is able to not only fulfill Andy's request, but also to provide guidance as to the prison yard, the personalities, the officials, and the ways of the environment. Red is a Playmaker.

## Befriend the Guardian Angels

Project managers often overlook the power of the administrative or executive assistants. In the vast majority of my projects, I need access to the key decision makers in the organization, which are oftentimes officers and C-level executives. You know, as well as I do, that that group does not manage their own calendar. If I want time with them, I need to work with their assistant. It is in the project's best interest, and therefore in mine, to be on exceptional terms with those assistants, whom I call the Guardian Angels. Chocolate? Wine? Small talk? Whatever it takes.

Now, please understand that I'm not talking straight-up bribery. Truly and genuinely get to know these folks. They are oftentimes being pulled in a number of directions, facing competing demands, and have to essentially manage the business life (and sometimes personal life) of that executive. In my experience, people can smell a rat a mile away. If you ooze in like a used car salesman, you probably are not going to get very far. Be genuine. Ask questions. Notice their environment. And above and beyond all else, be respectful of their time and the executive's time.

People want to feel valued, they want to be noticed, and they want to be appreciated. So how can you do that as the project manager? Show up at their desk demanding time on the boss' calendar, frustrated that everyone else does not value your project in all of its almighty splendid glory? No. Things like asking:

"How was your weekend?"

"You appear a little frazzled. Anything I can do to help?"

"I love that picture! Where were you when that was taken?"

And when they answer, actively listen to what they're saying and remember their answer the next time you see them. If you know they like coffee, bring them a cup from the cafeteria. Remember them when you close out your project by sending them a hand-written note thanking them for helping make your project a success.

## Be Aware of Personal Relationships

I worked for an organization that was known for nepotism and employed a lot of romantic and married couples. I did not fully consider that when engaging with some troubled stakeholders. Relatively new to the organization, I was still getting familiar with the individuals involved. After one particularly contentious and stressful meeting, I was cleaning up the conference room with the help of one of the quieter participants, Lisa. As she cleaned the white board, I took the opportunity to ask her about some of the other team members.

"Boy, that Jim Doyle sure gave me a run for my money. Is he always so difficult?" I asked.

"Yes, that's him. He's not known for winning friends, that's for sure" she replied.

Sensing that her and I had some common ground, and in the interest of developing a relationship with her, I continued, "honestly, he strikes me as a self-righteous douche-bag".

"If you think he's bad here, you should see how he is at home" she stated before walking out of the conference room.

Open mouth. Insert foot. My biggest lesson of that day, other than not to call people douche-bags, was to never assume that a relationship does not exist. Despite different last names, Jim and Lisa had been married for more than 10 years and despite stark differences in their personalities, they were very protective of each other.

So how do you get around this without directly asking? Earlier I mentioned the Playmaker. Identify who they are within your organization and get to know them. Get their sense of the organization, including who is connected to who.

## Negative Nancys

A word of warning on the Negative Nancys: they are individuals who may give the impression of being a Playmaker, yet they are bitter and jaded towards the organization. They know a lot, they talk a lot, but it tends to be negative and possibly somewhat aggressive. This is not the way to get things done nor is it in your best interest to align yourself with a Negative Nancy or Nelson. Whether you think it will or not, that negativity will impact your thoughts and possibly behaviors. In addition, you may be considered "guilty by association". Distance yourself from these folks.

I was facilitating a five-day class for the U.S. Air Force in which I had 25 senior airmen seated at tables in neatly organized rows. On the first day, the airman that was the closest to the door was sneezing and coughing, and he quickly declined as the day progressed. The next morning, the airman that was sitting in front of my sick student and two to the left of him, were all coughing and rapidly losing color and concentration. The next day the cycle progressed until on the fifth day, I only had nine airmen remaining in my class. (And yes, as soon as I caught on to the contagious nature of the bug, I was bathing in hand sanitizer and guzzling vitamin C!).

As goes the virus, so goes negativity. It spreads out of control. For every person that is touched, three to five more get infected. I have seen negativity and bad attitudes tear apart teams, halt progress, and turn an otherwise ideal project completely upside down.

## Make Ground Rules a Rule!

At the start of my career, I sought out tips and tricks, processes and procedures, that would make me a "better" project manager. I recognized the fact that I was young, and I was going to be in a position of leadership with people older and more experienced than I was. To me, research was how I strengthened my arsenal. One particular best practice that I found in those early days was the implementation of ground rules. Here is the critical aspect of ground rules, they are set by the project team, not the project manager, and it helps us understand our team members and what they value.

I was the project manager of a particularly nasty project: tight deadlines, long hours, and high stress all in a war room setting. I was in a male-dominated environment and my team included just two females, me and "Sue". Well, Sue had quite a reputation in the company and it was not a good one. She was known to be a complainer and was considered high maintenance. Honestly, people did not want to work with her, even though she possessed incredible technical knowledge. Many wondered if the only reason she was still employed was because the company feared legal repercussions if they fired her.

With slight apprehension, I told my team of gruff old-timers and Sue, that we would be documenting our team ground rules. I encouraged them to each contribute something to the ground rules and to be honest. I explained that the purpose was to understand the values of our team mates in order to develop our team norms and working agreements.

We progressed around the conference room:

"Schedule meetings to end five minutes early, so that we have time between meetings to tend to personal needs."

"Limit talking at a meeting to no more than five minutes for one individual to ensure time is not being monopolized."

"Do not cook fish in the microwave."

And then I got to Sue. At first, she did not want to participate, and I gave her a not-so-gentle nudge, letting her know that everyone was contributing.

"Ok, fine. I hate the use of the word 'guys'. I am not a guy, I am a woman. It really annoys me." A stunned silence fell over the room, and I noticed a few of the men roll their eyes. My first reaction was not exactly positive. After all, I was the mother of three daughters and I used the term 'guys' with them all the time, in a gender-neutral way. But I had to catch myself and acknowledge the fact that she just gave us an incredibly valuable little tid-bit about herself.

"Ok," I responded, "that is great to know Sue, because I know I use that all the time without considering gender. Now that I know it bothers you, I will do my best not to use it, but please extend me a little grace if I slip!" To which, she agreed.

Now here's the amazing thing about this situation. It could have gone badly very easily and further affirmed the men's not-so-nice perspective of Sue. But instead, an incredible thing happened. We began finding other words to use instead of "guys". Words like partners, buddies, giraffes, kumquats. It became silly and fun and almost like a game.

Sue lightened up and I saw her start to engage more in the project. After one particularly productive meeting, I wondered how it would have been different had we not identified that that one simple word had a negative impact on her. She probably would have appeared sullen and angry, feeling as though she was being disrespected. But having us be aware of it, whether we agreed or not, enabled us to almost visibly lift a weight off her shoulders.

And this story has a happy ending. The project was delivered on-time and on-budget. Sue was nominated as the MVP of the project and went on to have a wonderful career at the company. Now I don't know if I can claim credit for the turnaround because I had them use ground rules, but it certainly confirmed to me that people want to be understood. Developing and implementing team ground rules is one of the easiest ways to learn about your team.

# Chapter 2 Action Plan

My key takeaways and "Ah-has!" from this chapter:

_____

_____

_____

Why these takeaways are important:

_____

_____

_____

Target dates for implementation:

_____

_____

_____

# Chapter 3

# Communication

As Steven Covey famously proclaimed, "most people do not listen with the intent to understand; they listen with the intent to reply."

That statement is straight up, unpolished, truth. While this is a frequent occurrence, more frequent than not, it is not necessarily because we are consciously choosing to not listen effectively. Formulating our response in our mind before it is time for us to talk is a basic human behavior. We talk slower than we comprehend. What that means is that part of our brain is "checking out" of listening and has already filled in the blanks and finished the statements of the other person. Our brain is incredibly adept at assessing a situation even if there are missing pieces. Here is a great example of that phenomena:

*I cnduo't bvleiee taht I culod aulaclty uesdtannrd waht I was rdnaieg. Unisg the icndeblire pweor of the hmuan mnid, aocdcrnig to rseecrah at Cmabrigde Uinervtisy, it dseno't mttaer in waht oderr the lterets in a wrod are, the olny irpoamtnt tihng is taht the frsit and lsat ltteer be in the rhgit pclae. The rset can be a taotl mses and you can sitll raed it whoutit a pboerlm. Tihs is bucseae the huamn mnid deos not raed ervey ltteer by istlef, but the wrod as a wlohe. Aaznmig, huh? Yaeh and I awlyas tghhuot slelinpg was ipmorantt! See if yuor fdreins can raed tihs too.*

Learning to slow down and focus on the speaker takes deliberate practice. Obviously, environmental influences can impact our ability to listen effectively. As a project manager, if you feel like you are being pressured about your project, you're under stress, or if you have a conflict situation, your brain is going to be in overdrive trying to "protect" you from these perceived attacks of a challenging conversation. The protection mechanism is to be completely reactionary. Respond and defend!

Here are some tips for listening effectively:

1. Provide feedback to the speaker periodically throughout the conversation. This may be simple body language gestures, as in nodding your head and making eye contact or small words or phrases, such as "ok.." or "I see…" or "tell me more".

2. Really try to place yourself in their shoes and empathize with their feelings, their challenges, and their positions. Emotional maturity is displayed when you can feel that empathy while disagreeing with why they are feeling those feelings. Just because you do not understand or agree does not mean you cannot be compassionate.

3. At appropriate spots in the conversation, ask questions to encourage them to continue and to demonstrate to them that you care enough to want to learn more. There is nothing worse than when you are sharing something with someone and you are greeted with a blank stare. People need engagement and encouragement.

4. Remember to listen to understand and not to respond. Do not aggressively seek a hint of a break in their talking so that you can talk. Allow for an actual moment, a few breaths, to be sure they are done or are pausing, and then begin to speak. Being interrupted simply sends the message that the listener feels their opinions and their words are more important and more valuable.

5. Sometimes people just need to vent. They are not looking for you to solve their problems. Be very cautious with offering solutions in situations where they were not specifically requested. If you are not sure if they are looking for solutions from you, ask them! Unsolicited problem solving can leave the speaker feeling that perhaps they were not smart enough or capable enough to solve the problem on their own. Look for openings such as "how do you think I should handle this?" or "what would you do in this situation?".

6. And possibly the most important tip for effective listening is to NOT make it about you. Do not look for opportunities to compare their situation to your own. "Oh, you are struggling with your workload? Me too, man, I'm jammed up! We're trying to

remodel the house, the kids have soccer, and I still haven't done my taxes!". Not a good way to ingratiate yourself to the speaker.

## The Power of Our Words

I recently connected with a gentleman at an industry meeting and he invited me to discuss a possible business relationship and consider any synergies we share. He asked me to give him my "5-minute" resume, which I did. His 5-minute resume, which took 15 minutes, was punctuated and framed with dollar values:

"I painted house numbers on curbs and made $540,000. I went on to purchase land for $80,000. With some creative thinking, I split the parcel and ended up selling it for $790,000. After that I purchased another large parcel and sold that in exchange for two $3.5 million mansions."

After he so eloquently presented his resume, he asked me what stood out the most to me from what he said.

"Your overuse of dollar values in describing your business experience" I offered. It was as if I had slapped him across the face.

"Most people want to know where I got the stencils to paint the curb" he remarked.

"I have no interest in painting curbs."

While his accomplishments were certainly laudable, and I listened intently to his presentation, my objective in meeting with him was to determine if our business pursuits were synergistic.

While no one ever complains about making money, it came across to me that this was his sole focus. While his intention may have been to simply illustrate that he is a successful businessman, what I heard was that the most important aspect of business was making money.

What do your words say about you?

## Body Language

The classic scene from the Little Mermaid gives us a visual into body language. Ariel has just signed over her voice to the sea witch, Ursula, in exchange for human legs to pursue her prince:

*You'll have your looks!*
*Your pretty face!*
*And don't underestimate the importance of body language!*
*Ha!*

*- Lyrics from The Little Mermaid*
*Music and Lyrics by Alan Menken and Howard Ashman*

To Ursula's credit, she had a point about body language. We oftentimes convey much more with our body than we do with our words. Tone of voice, inflection, eye contact, eye rolls, distractions – they all play a role in how our message is received.

I was the manager over a very driven, high-performing team. We all worked well together and enjoyed a great relationship. My highest performing team member, Tracy, had joined me in my office for her weekly 1-on-1.

I asked her to share her project updates and while she was talking, I turned sideways to look at and respond to some emails on my computer. With no warning, she hit the desk with her hand, exclaiming, "This is my time with you. Please focus on me right now, not your email."

I literally jumped out of my seat and quite honestly, I felt as though I had been slapped across my face. It was exactly the wake-up call I needed. I had been taken advantage of our friendly relationship and was not giving my employees the respect, consideration, and focus that was appropriate as their manager.

Although her reaction stung, I immediately recognized how critical it was that she took that step. I immediately apologized and thanked her, profusely, for being honest with me about how it made her feel when I behaved in a distracted manner. And consider this: this scenario played out 15 years ago, before smart phones. I had a Blackberry but did not even look at it while I was at the office. Today, we cannot take two steps without looking at our phone.

Because of this confrontation, I have mindfully focused on clearing my environment and distractions whenever I meet with my team members and stakeholders. I place my phone on silent and turn it over so that I do not see messages pop-up. Even a shift of an eye to an email notification can convey the message that the email is more important than the other party in the conversation.

## Eye Contact

Eye contact can be a little tricky: too much eye contact and the other person feels uncomfortable, too little eye contact and the other person feels like you are not engaged. Periodically catching the eye of the speaker lets them know that you are actively listening.

The visual dominance ratio considers the amount of time that you are making eye contact during communication. If you spend as much time looking the other person in the eye as you do looking away, your visual dominance ratio would be around a 1.0.

Spending more time looking away than looking at the other person would result in a visual dominance ratio that is less than 1.0. If you spend more time looking at the person than looking away, your visual dominance ratio is greater than one.

Why is the visual dominance ratio important to you, as a project manager? Psychologists have demonstrated that individuals with a high visual dominance ratio are considered the "bosses" or in the superior role. Those with a visual dominance ratio less than one are considered the "employees".

As project managers, our goal is to be collaborative and be confident. If we are spending more time looking away, we can come across as having a lack of confidence or as inferior. But gazing a bit too long at the face of our communication partner can be intimidating and give the impression of superiority. If the individual feels inferior to you, they may not be open and honest in their communication.

## The Question of Questions

Asking questions can be one of the most powerful additions to communication. The asking of questions can reap a rich harvest of information while also providing a number of other benefits. Practice asking open-ended questions that will allow the person to provide context and clarity and present their position.

Be cautious, however, of asking questions that take the conversation off from the speaker's original trajectory:

I was meeting with the sponsor of my project for the first time, in somewhat of a get-to-know-you session. While I wanted to keep it conversational, I also recognized that her time was extremely limited, and the project had tight constraints.

We began with the typical formalities and she asked me to tell her about myself and my experience at the organization. As I begin to tell her about a project I did for the convention in Vegas, she starts questioning me about Vegas. And gambling. And the heat. And the crowds. And then travel. And international travel. And the suitcases I use.

I did my best to rein it in, but she was persistent. Her line of questioning was not only distracting, it was frustrating. If I refused to answer the questions, I feared she would be offended or put off. Allowing the conversation to veer off track, however, impacted my ability to get and give the necessary information for the project.

Recognizing our time constraints, I responded "I would love to talk with you more about travel. I love to travel and would love to hear your experiences. Maybe we could meet for coffee next week?" The message was conveyed, and we were able to redirect the conversation back to the topic at hand: the project.

## Benefits of Listening

I will readily admit it. I was, and still am, a horrible listener. But in consolation, I am not alone. Great listeners are few and far between. I must really work at, and practice, active and patient listening. Slowing down and being mindful and conscious of connecting with the speaker. This includes being very aware of my body language, my eye contact, and my questioning and encouragement.

Why is this so important to you, as a project manager? Our job is often mockingly referred to as "herding cats" or "nailing Jell-O to a wall". We are task masters, driving change, enforcing constraints, and managing multiple personalities. All of those implications are improved by being a skillful listener.

Active listening leads to:

**Respect.** When people feel listened to, they feel respected. Respect is typically met with respect in return. As project managers, we oftentimes manage without authority. When the folks that we are working with respect us, we are more likely to be functioning in a collaborative environment, despite the fact that we do not have full authority.

**Strong relationships.** As we listen to our team members and our stakeholders, we get to know them on a different level. Little nuances, comments, or reactions can provide us with insight into how that person ticks. This awareness allows the relationships to grow and flourish. We need to move beyond seeing people as just a means to an end, and instead value their unique role, experiences, and contributions. Strong relationships are critical to project success.

**Synergy.** I have a theory that if you talked to 100 people with different opinions than your own, you would likely be able to find some common ground, some common interest, some shared belief. Society today has programmed us that we are so different from each other, but I do not believe that is true. When we begin to actively listen to our team members and stakeholders, we are able to discover those synergies.

I was leading a very high-stress difficult project in India. After a few weeks of very long hours, the core team was able to sit and decompress together. I looked around the group and realized how interesting our make-up was: a Christian, a Muslim, a Hindu, an atheist, and a Catholic. But that is not how I saw them – they were just my friends and team mates. We started discussing our belief systems, our influences, and our cultures and it was an incredibly rich dialog. We could do that because we trusted each other, and we listened to each other.

**Creativity and innovation.** Last, but certainly not least, when we listen and engage actively with our team members and stakeholders, we spark creativity and innovation. The verse regarding "iron sharpens iron" comes into play. When you are able to effectively collaborate, through active listening, you will discover significantly more potential and creative ideas than one person can conceive on their own.

# Chapter 3 Action Plan

My key takeaways and "Ah-has!" from this chapter:

_____

_____

_____

Why these takeaways are important:

_____

_____

_____

Target dates for implementation:

_____

_____

_____

# Chapter 4

# Spend It Like It's Your Money

As I mentioned previously, my parents owned a large child care facility, both working 24/7 to ensure it was a success and they were able to support our family with it. Costs were always a consideration as margins were slim. Everything mattered: a staff member staying an extra 30 minutes, 12 Cheez-Its versus 10, wasted construction paper if the project materials were cut incorrectly, or keeping the heat on in the building after we closed.

I was able to see and feel the direct impact of money in and money out. That experience gave me a unique experience when I entered the corporate environment. I treated every penny spent as my own money, as though it was coming from my pocket. Because in a way, it was.

Oftentimes, we forget, or maybe even choose not to believe, that every action we take in an organization has an impact on the company's bottom-line. It is time to shift our perspective from "what is the company doing for me?" to "what can I do to enable my company to be successful?". The more successful our organization is, the greater the likelihood for trickle down positive impacts.

## Everything Counts: Resources

Every hour we spend or don't spend contributing has a cost. In project work, it is important to always consider not only the resource hours that will be needed for the project, but also the opportunity cost of taking those resources away from other work.

I was a Director of Project Management for a large financial services firm. My Vice President and I met to review some potential upcoming projects. There were two that were under consideration for me to personally manage. Costs were a leading factor in project selection. I was known to be extremely diligent when it came to project costs.

Mr. VP presents both projects to me and tells me "I wanted to have you take a look at both of them, although I am assuming you are going to want to go with Project A because it is 'cheaper'".

Project A was a project that was going to be handled completely internally whereas Project B was going to include the use of vendors and there was an equipment purchase. Looking at the two projects side-by-side, Project A certainly did appear to be the cheaper project.

However, upon closer analysis, it was evident to me that Project A was going to require approximately ten times the number of hours from myself, whereas Project B would require minimal oversight. Because this organization did not track internal resource hours or cost, to Mr. VP, he did not appreciate the final impact.

I quantified my time on both projects using a loaded resource rate (considering salary and benefits) and then also used a rough estimate of the opportunity cost of taking me away from some other key initiatives. By doing so, based on the financials, it was apparent that Project B was the better option if cost was the number one consideration.

Just because your organization does not track internal resource costs does not mean it should not be considered. As a project manager, you should not only be factoring that in on your projects, you should also look for opportunities to help educate and inform the organization: even though resources are not directly billed to the project, every hour spent on any work is a cost to the company.

## Everything Counts: Materials and Equipment

Do you have a corporate credit card? How much authority do you have with that card? For some project managers, the allure of the corporate card can almost feel like a blank check. There have been many expense reports across my desk for purchases that, quite honestly, the project manager would not have made if the money was coming from their pocket.

While I am not opposed to spending and supporting my team to enable an environment where they can be successful, I always check myself and my team members on the necessity of any purchase. If there is a compelling business case, then certainly it can be pursued.

I had recently assumed the leadership of a team that was broken and dysfunctional, in all honesty. Creating a team identity was a high priority for me: I needed to improve the cohesiveness, trust, and engagement as quickly as possible or I would have to consider the option of eliminating people from the team.

We worked together to "re-brand" the team, including a new name, new acronym (of course!), and a new logo. To literally wrap them in our team identity, I purchased professional shirts with the team logo and a banner that hung over our work area. While some may consider this a waste of money, I wanted my team members to always know that they were part of our team. It made a huge difference to all of us.

In another instance, I was the Scrum Master for a relatively 'agile-mature' team. This high-functioning team had been regularly improving velocity (their measurable productivity) and had eight sprints (or iterations) completed. As is appropriate for a Scrum Master, I was focused on improving velocity of the team. Though their velocity seemed to have leveled off, I sought ways to continue to improve it without expecting my team to work longer hours or in more stressful conditions.

During our post-sprint retrospective, I asked the team if there was anything I could do or change for them that would allow them to improve their productivity. They really struggled with their current computer monitors and felt that if they were upgraded, their productivity would improve. I asked them to quantify the productivity improvement in terms of the increase in velocity. The team agreed on a measurement and committed to achieving that new velocity if I was able to secure the new monitors.

This organization was not particularly open to equipment purchases, but I was able to provide a compelling argument by quantifying the impact of the improved productivity as compared to the cost of the monitors. Based on my analysis it would only take two sprints for the organization to "earn" back the investment. With an estimated 20 sprints remaining, this seemed a worthy investment.

My reputation for being financially conservative once again played in my favor. If I was asking for an investment in equipment, I must truly believe that it was worth it. My team received their new monitors and staying true to their word, their velocity increased even beyond what they had originally promised.

Spending money, in and of itself, is not necessarily bad, there just must be an assessment of the value or return on investment. Do not discount, as well, the credibility and reputation you build as a project manager that carefully considers costs. When you are financially responsible, the leadership of your organization is more likely to trust you and approve funding requests.

## Everything Counts: Travel

Oh, the joys of business travel, right?! While there certainly can be some perks, if you travel a lot as a project manager you certainly recognize the negative aspects, as well. I have such a vivid memory of my first international flight for business. It was in the 90s and the company policy was that we could fly business class when traveling internationally.

Large, comfortable seats and exemplary service were just the tip of the ice berg. I was treated to a lovely meal, a choice of high-end wines, and the ultimate treat was dessert: an ice cream cart ripe with your pick of decadent toppings. As a kid that grew up in a small town in Maine, this trip to London seemed like a luxurious dream.

Since the 90s, certain perks have been reduced, not only from a company travel policy perspective, but also the airlines themselves. Business class on airlines today is certainly not the business class of 20 years ago.

Let's be honest, business travel may seem glamorous to those on the outside, but for us road warriors it can be anything but glamorous. Late flights, lost luggage, bad hotel rooms, not to mention the time away from our family, friends, and our own bed can leave us run-down and cranky! So, is it a bad thing to want to spring for a little splurge here and there on the company?

Just like food, wine, and fun, it is not bad in moderation. Are the purchases enabling you to be more effective at your job? Or possibly, intangibly, is it improving your loyalty to the company that will be played out as increased performance?

I was a member of a project team that would be working in India for four weeks. While we flew coach domestically, the international flights were business class. This allowed us to relax and sleep, arriving in India ready to go. While there was certainly a cost associated with those tickets as compared to flying coach, the intangibles were certainly worth it. I cannot say I would be compelled to take that trip if I knew I was spending 18 hours in a cramped economy seat.

At the end of that same project in India, the team went out to a celebratory dinner at the hotel. We had worked hard, an extreme number of hours, and we accomplished all of our goals. We were in desperate need of a celebration! I was the project manager over the training component of the project, and 'Betsy' was the overall project manager.

Betsy, like myself, was known for being very focused and strict on proper project spending. She had provided every team member with a very strict spending budget for their time in India.

At the celebration dinner, a few bottles of wine were ordered for the table. Given that there were nine of us dining, two bottles did not go very far. When the waiter returned to the table, he suggested another bottle to one of my team leads, 'John'. John looked at it on the wine list, considered the price (in rupees), and agreed to the recommendation.

A few minutes later, the waiter returned with the bottle of wine, showing it off to John for approval. With great pomp and circumstance, he prepared the bottle of wine with the flair of a 5-star sommelier. We were all quite surprised, entertained and amused by the show as the other bottles of wine had not been prepared in the same manner.

A few of us enjoyed a glass and chatted about returning to the States in the morning, celebrating a project that really performed well. Our celebration came to a quick stop when the bill arrived. Apparently, there is a big difference between 1,250 rupees as compared to 12,500 rupees.

What John thought was about a $20 bottle of wine was actually a $200 bottle of wine. After the shock and dismay, we all broke out into a fit of laughter, finally understanding why we were treated to such a royal show in the preparation of the wine. Poor John! For a moment, I thought he might actually cry.

But we were a team. We had successfully completed one of the most challenging projects because of our strength as a team, so this was certainly not going to be any different. We each evaluated how much we had spent of our meal allowances, calculating how much we had left over. Splitting it up amongst the team allowed us to "absorb" the bottle of wine and still stay within our budget.

Betsy's attention to costs on the project impacted and influenced our behavior and our spending to ensure that we stayed within compliance. Although there was some grumbling when the allowances were originally discussed, we all felt pretty good about the fact that we enjoyed a very nice bottle of wine as our final celebration, and still stayed within the budget.

And the coolest thing? We saved the bottle and every team member signed the label. I still have that bottle on my office shelf. That bottle represents team work and it represents success.

A couple of other key points on travel:

- If you are responsible for making your own travel arrangements, take the time to shop around for the best value. I always consider location, cleanliness, and WIFI as my three must-haves.

- Take advantage of pre-payment discounts on hotel rooms

- Evaluate your transportation needs and do not overlook parking fees. A black car or executive car service can prove to be cheaper and more efficient than a rental car in higher priced cities. Uber and Lyft are also alternatives to renting.

- Many hotels offer free breakfast and some even have a free evening reception.

- Most importantly, when you travel on business do your best to make decisions as you would if you were spending your own money.

# Chapter 4 Action Plan

My key takeaways and "Ah-has!" from this chapter:

_____

_____

_____

Why these takeaways are important:

_____

_____

_____

Target dates for implementation:

_____

_____

_____

# Chapter 5

# Predict, Prepare, Present

The only two certains in life are death and taxes. And the only certainty in project management is risk or uncertainty. Regardless of the type of project, your project environment, or even your project management expertise, risk is inherent to all project endeavors. You are, after all, creating something unique within limited constraints.

This risk awareness is an important component of project management maturity. And once you understand that as a project manager, you must be able to convey that reality to your stakeholders.

My first real corporate project was a 5-year project. The second day on the job, I was asked to provide the date of delivery and the project cost. Not an estimate, mind you. The actual date and dollar amount. Under protest, I provided a target date and budget, while trying to set the expectation that a lot could change between that day and the final launch.

That was over twenty years ago, and the pace of change has dramatically increased. With the accelerating pace of change comes increased risk and uncertainty. Now my projects are typically no more than 6 – 9 months in length for more control.

## Clairvoyant or Just a Good Project Manager?

Can you predict the likelihood of your project delivering on time, on budget, and with the value that was needed? What does that prediction look like today? Next week? Next month? As risks are realized, fluctuations occur in the environment, and people perform differently than expected, you, as the project manager, should be able to articulate the impact.

I love watching HGTV and the various home remodeling shows such as Fixer Upper, Property Brothers, Flip or Flop, and Love it or List It. For all of these shows, the premise is that the "professional" remodelers give a budget and timeline for the requested renovations. As a project manager, I admit that I experience many cringe-worthy moments while watching:

- They give estimates of time and cost without in-depth inspection and analysis of the property
- Contingency is occasionally discussed but it is not quantitatively calculated based on known risks
- Knob and tube wiring, foundation issues, asbestos, and lead paint all seem to make an appearance on every show, yet somehow the remodelers are taken by surprise each time!

Of course, these shows are made for television and they do a pretty good job of illustrating the concepts of constraints. "Oh, you want the in-floor heating now? Ok, then we can't do the new fireplace."

How do they predict the costs and budget with relative accuracy? Two main factors: the projects are short-term, usually less than three months. The projects are also squarely within their realm of experience in a relatively controlled environment. Being able to predict the project outcome is mandatory for those renovation programs to be successful.

## Remember the Motto: Always be Prepared

At any point in your project, you should know your project's story. What are you most concerned with? What aspects are going well? If there was a disruption tomorrow, what are the impacts?

Picture this: you are at leadership meeting and suddenly the sponsor asks you to give an update on your project. Because you know your numbers, your variances, and your trends, you are able to easily convey the current status. When asked about the impacts of potential changes, you are able to respond intelligently. Make that scenario a reality by knowing your data.

In agile, we talk about the Scrum Master being "obsessed with velocity": always looking at how to boost productivity without compromising your team or your quality. Become a project manager that is obsessed with your project. To the point, in fact, that at any moment you can answer questions about your project with relative ease and accuracy.

There are six main tools that I use to stay obsessed with my projects, three that are data driven and three that are documents:

**Project baselines.** Regardless of the complexity or even maturity of my project, I always capture a scope, a schedule, and a cost baseline. These baselines are my measuring sticks for project progress. In addition, I use my baselines to manage my stakeholders' expectations. When there are variances from those baselines, I communicate those variances, including the causes of the variances and the proposed actions, to the stakeholders.

Research has demonstrated that no news is worse that bad news. Keeping the stakeholders in the loop on the progress against baselines and the variances, gives them insight and manages their expectations in a timely manner. Even if it is not good news or the news they were hoping to receive.

**Trends.** Monitoring the project progress against the baselines will identify the variances. Those variances tracked over time will yield project trending data. Leveraging trending data positions you to "predict" the future of your project. While there will always be a certain amount of random or predictable variance, identify special causes of variances and how those special causes impact the trends.

The trending data allows you to forecast more accurately which lends to better stakeholder expectation management. In addition, you will be proactive in implementing preventive actions to reverse any negative trends. When you actively manage the stakeholder expectations and implement proactive actions, you will be viewed as reliable and in control. This will, in turn, increase the stakeholders' trust in you. And that's a good thing!

**Past project files.** Do not believe the saying that lightning does not strike twice in the same location because it certainly does! One of your greatest, and frequently overlooked, tools that you have is your past project files. Use the past to predict the future. If 90% of all projects in the last two years came in 20% over budget, there is a good chance that your project will be over budget.

If your organization does not have a method of archiving and retrieving historical project information, create something, even if it's just an archive of just your project files. Past project performance, realized risks, issues, changes, and resource records should all be taken into consideration.

**Issue log**. One of my most frequently consulted project documents is my issue log. It is the focus of my day-to-day project management, ensuring that I am applying my resources to the highest priority concerns.

As with trending data, the issue log is critical in managing stakeholder expectations. At a minimum, the issue log will include an issue ID, a clear and concise description (written in layman terms with minimal acronyms), an assigned owner, current status, and a target date for resolution. The issue log should be transparent and accessible to the project team and select stakeholders.

**Change log**. While in predictive projects, change is perceived as the enemy, change is going to happen. Having a solid change control process ensures that all proposed changes are managed, evaluated, and responded to appropriately. At a minimum, the change log details the date the change was submitted, the submitter, the type of change, description of the change, whether the change was approved or denied, and the impact of the change.

If a change has been requested but denied, the original requestor needs to be notified of that. I have witnessed situations where someone asked for a change and when they did not hear anything back from the team or the project manager, assumed that the change was implemented. Imagine the disappointment at project launch when their change was not included. As with the other tools, the change log is integral in managing the stakeholder expectations.

**Risk register**. The sister to the issue log is the risk register. This is another main tool for the day-to-day management of the project. A project risk is defined as an uncertain event that if it occurs will have an impact on the project. Managing risk allows you to not only be proactive with responses but to also have a good understanding of the likelihood of achieving the project objectives.

The risk register includes, at a minimum, the risk ID, the name of the risk, a clearly written description of the risk, the probability and impact scores for the risk, the assigned risk owner, the risk response, any triggers, and potentially a quantitative assessment of the risk in terms of cost and/or schedule impact.

With numerical probability and impact scores, it is possible to then calculate an overall risk score: for each risk, multiply probability by the impact to arrive at the risk score; sum the risk scores and divide by the overall number of risks to get to the project risk score. As this analysis is repeated throughout the project, the overall project risk score should be decreasing. Generally speaking, projects are risk declining models.

## Present with Confidence

*"Communicate and over-communicate to your customers and stakeholders! They shouldn't have to ask where you are with your project. They should know before that's ever a question."*
*Sarah Rexrode*

Remember the scenario I mentioned earlier where you are put on the spot and asked to provide an update on your project? Does the very thought of that scenario set your heart to racing and your palms to sweating? Anxiety related to public speaking is attributed to, at least in part, how confident you are with your materials, information, and what you are about to share. The more confident you are, the less anxiety you will experience.

Now of course, even with confidence, your nerves can certainly get the best of you. As a project manager you want to portray confidence, expertise, and control in presenting your project data. If you do not seem confident and credible in the delivery of the project information, how do you expect the stakeholders to trust the information that you are providing?

I recommend connecting with a speaking group or organization to help with your technique and delivery. I belong to the National Speakers Association (NSA). While it may not seem to be an evident connection, as project managers, we are speaking and presenting to groups throughout our projects. While you may not qualify as a professional member, you can join as a candidate member. Local chapters typically have a monthly meeting with expert speakers presenting.

Another option is to join Toastmasters. Not only will you get training on presentation, style, and communication techniques, you are afforded the opportunity to practice presenting and receive feedback. While you may not love speaking in public, look for opportunities to do just that. The more you practice, the easier it becomes.

Presenting project information effectively also means that you have the ability to read your audience. You need to find that delicate balance between too much information and not enough information; too much emotion and not enough emotion; and pessimism, realism, and optimism. The goal is to provide enough information to keep people interested and engaged while avoiding flooding them with unnecessary information that will make them freak out or check out.

If you feel put on the spot while presenting, here are a couple of responses to preserve your credibility:

1. "That's a great question, Bob! I actually want to verify my information before responding. I'll get back to you later today on that."

2. "Great question/comment/suggestion, Sue! What do the rest of you think about what she asked/said/suggested?"

3. "Perhaps you could re-phrase that, Gerald, as I am not sure I quite understood the question."

4. "That's a good question, Brittany! I'd be interested in hearing your preliminary thoughts on the situation before I respond."

To convey confidence, be aware of making qualifying statements. These qualifiers oftentimes serve to discredit the information that is to follow.

For example:

"This may be a dumb idea, but what about....?"

Or

"I'm not sure if this is important or relevant, but..."

Or

"I may be totally off base with this, but I was thinking..."

The use of qualifying statements tends to be more prevalent with women, but men are certainly not immune to doing it in situations where they feel uncertain or intimidated. During your next meeting, be conscious of the use of qualifying statements, both by yourself and others.

## A Picture is Worth a Thousand Words

People are busy. They are inundated with a constant stream of information. Make it easy for your stakeholders and team members to understand the project status or situation by using clear, colored pictures. This is one of the reasons I consider a work breakdown structure (WBS) to be a best practice. People may not read a detailed scope statement, but they can look at a WBS and understand exactly what is included (and what is not included) in the project.

Whenever possible, create a visual representation of the status of your project. Control or run charts can visually depict trending data. Red, yellow, green indicators can relay issue and risk status. Any type of graphic that you believe will help convey the information should be explored. At that same time, you do not want your presentation to look like a comic strip or that clip art vomited on PowerPoint. Again, it's a delicate balance.

A mature project manager:

- *Predicts* where the project is going by using their knowledge of the project and relevant data sources and indicators.
- *Prepares* information based on current data and trends that captures the project situation in a manner that is easy to understand and conveys the appropriate message.
- *Presents* credible, timely and engaging information consistently to maximize stakeholder engagement and manage the stakeholders' expectations.

# Chapter 5 Action Plan

My key takeaways and "Ah-has!" from this chapter:

_____

_____

_____

Why these takeaways are important:

_____

_____

_____

Target dates for implementation:

_____

_____

_____

# Chapter 6

# Leadership and Teamwork

It used to be that project management was nothing more than task management. Project management was concerned with leveraging technical expertise, putting activities into a schedule, and then making sure the workers got it done. The days of the micro-manager / task manager are gone, and a new style of leadership is required.

When you think of a skilled and effective leader, who comes to mind? Are they someone in your immediate circle, such as a parent or boss? Are they a political figure? Are they a historic leader? What are the characteristics, traits, and approaches that make them stand out to you as a leader?

Now consider yourself. Do you view yourself as a leader or as a manager? How does your team view you?

Leadership and management are very different concepts and approaches. As a project manager, yes, we manage. But we also need to lead. We are instrumental in facilitating change within the organization. That change, in turn, leads to strategic growth. Ultimately project management is critical to an organization's success.

## Motivational leader

*"Don't forget that behind a great project, is great people. Make sure your people have what they need to be successful, both personally and professionally." Jeremiah*

Being a compelling leader enables you to bring out the best in your team members, your stakeholders, and your organization. Think about your idea of a good leader and consider their behaviors. Leaders model the behavior that want to see.

I was having a casual conversation with a co-worker about a new sponsor, "Ron", that I was going to be working with on an upcoming project. Knowing that she had worked with him before, I asked her for feedback on him. "Ron's either the best guy to work with or the worst guy to work with. Depends on the day." Come to find out, Ron was known for being temperamental with notorious mood swings. Before approaching him in the morning, his team would wait to feel out which "Ron" showed up that day. The inconsistency in his behaviors did not instill confidence in his leadership capabilities.

In addition to being emotional stable, a motivational leader inspires trust by backing and defending their team. To err is human and there will always be situations and scenarios where a team member will make a mistake. A true leader will acknowledge the mistake and work with the individual privately to remedy the situation. Calling out a team member or playing the blame game damages the team cohesiveness and betrays the team trust.

Above all else, believe in your team. This will inspire them and motivate them to do well and to meet their goals. Princeton conducted an interesting research study using lab mice and human subjects. They had two groups of participants: one study group was told that their mice had been bred to be very adept at navigating mazes for a reward. The other group was advised that their mice were just regular mice with no special training.

The group with the "special" mice reported significantly higher levels of achievement as compared to the other group with normal mice.

That could be expected, except for the fact that neither group of mice were specially trained. In truth, all the mice were exactly the same. What could explain the performance difference? Was it the managers' higher expectations of those mice they thought could succeed? After all, the mice were the same in both test groups. Believe your team is successful and they will be successful.

A motivational leader is also not only open to new ideas, they seek out and encourage new ideas, innovation, and creativity. They are not afraid to challenge the status quo and recognize that creativity and innovation is necessary for business growth and success.

If you have been in project management for a number of years or even with your organization for a while, you may have settled into a comfortable position of habit. Guess what? It's time to get uncomfortable and get away from the status quo. Seek out new ideas for accomplishing the goals and tasks of the project. And do not be afraid to have fun.

# Servant leadership

*"Operating as a servant-leader should be a requirement -- In many organizations, the PM operates as coordinator; and yet has the responsibility of the project's success or failure -- and empathizing with the team-member/stakeholder provides the much-needed governance in achieving project's success/goal." J. Chukwudi Osakwe*

Buh-bye command-and-control and hello servant leadership! Today's workforce is not your mama's workforce. In the information age, knowledge workers dominate, and they do not want to be micromanaged. Our team members are looking for challenging, inspired, and collaborative work environments.

Robert K. Greenleaf once said, "Good leaders must first become good servants." A servant leader focuses primarily on the needs of others, and in doing so, becomes a leader through behaviors, considerations, and actions versus through power and position. Servant leaders put the needs of others first, share power, and help people develop.

In project management, the concept of servant leadership was brought to the forefront with agile project management. In agile project management, the scrum master focuses on clearing impediments from the team and is obsessed with increasing team velocity (productivity during each sprint or iteration). Status reporting is shared during daily stand-up meetings during which each team member shares what they did yesterday, what they are doing today, and any impediments to getting their work done. This is where the scrum master focuses their efforts: removing those things that are preventing the team from maximizing their productivity.

Take a few minutes to consider servant leadership within your environment. Would you consider your manager a servant leader? Why or why not? Would your team consider you a servant leader? Why or why not? Would your team benefit from servant leadership?

## There is no "I" in TEAM

You know what they say: "teamwork makes the dream work!". If you have not yet realized that your project is dependent upon teamwork and collaboration, then consider this your wake-up call.

*"The best project I worked on was a data archival and migration project. It was very successful due to a strong team cohesion. The team was co-located and continuously cross-training one another as time allowed. It was a very motivating*

*environment and ended up supporting the career goals of many team members." Matthew Hall*

Recognizing that you are all in it together, allows your team to feed off of the support and innovation. It is helpful to understand Tuckman's Ladder and the stages of team development.

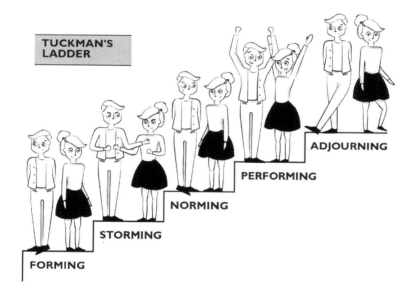

The forming stage begins when the team meets and learns about the project, their roles and responsibilities. At this point, the team members are functioning in isolation and are not as open with each other. As project manager, it is important to create an environment where the team members

81

can network and get to know each other personally. Leveraging some type of an ice breaker can be helpful. The forming stage is especially challenging for virtual teams.

In the storming stage, the environment can become destructive and counterproductive. The team members are not working collaboratively and may not open to differing ideas and perspectives. Team members are often defensive in this stage. You will need to be more hands-on during this stage, guiding your team to resolve their conflicts and breaking down barriers that exist.

After a while, the team settles in to the norming stage, working together and adjusting work habits and behaviors to support the team, increasing their trust. Work may be occurring independently with each team member contributing "their piece." At this stage, you should be able to back off a bit from your oversight, allowing the team to grow, develop, and increase their momentum.

Ideally, your team reaches the performing stage. In this stage, they are a well-organized team and are interdependent, working through issues smoothly and effectively. This illustrates the concept of synergy where the sum is greater than the individual parts. In my experience, truly "performing" teams are the result of an inspired leader, typically a servant leader.

Once the project is done, the team, of course, adjourns and moves on to their next assignment.

Know your team, know what stage they are in, and know what motivates them as people. I have always said that I would take someone with the 'will' any day over the 'skill'. I can teach the skill, but it is difficult to change the will.

If you are struggling with team motivation, use your detective skills to find out the root cause. It is amazing what you will learn and discover about your team members when you actually talk to them.

When I assumed the leadership of the struggling corporate training team, I knew I had one major at-risk performer, Alicia. Although she appeared very capable, her performance was lackluster, and she was just not engaged. I asked Alicia about her future goals and was fascinated to learn that she wanted to go to nursing school, get her R.N., and eventually become a nurse practitioner.

Alicia's face lit up when she talked about nursing and she became animated and excited. It was like a completely different side to her. Grabbing onto her energy and enthusiasm, I asked her how I could assist her in achieving her goals.

After some discussion, we were able to agree on a split-schedule that would allow her to keep her job with me while also attending nursing school. She was ecstatic and immediately started her application paperwork to the local school. I kept tabs on her admissions process, demonstrating that I was truly in her corner. Her performance blossomed, and she quickly became recognized as one of our best contributors.

This situation took place in 2005 and I left the company to start PM Learning Solutions in 2007. A few years ago, I was attending a community event when I heard my name being called across the crowd. I was thrilled to see Alicia after all these years.

After a nice hug and exchange of pleasantries, she excitedly told me that she was now a nurse practitioner. "And," she exclaimed, "I owe it all to you. You not only believed in me, you created a path for me to succeed. I cannot begin to tell you how grateful I am that you took over our team back then!". Ok, yes, I may have cried a little bit.

# Chapter 6 Action Plan

My key takeaways and "Ah-has!" from this chapter:

_____

_____

_____

Why these takeaways are important:

_____

_____

_____

Target dates for implementation:

_____

_____

_____

# Chapter 7

# Put Things in Perspective

I took my work personally. Very personally. Perhaps it was my upbringing. I was raised in a small business household. My parents worked together at the business and my employment at that business was just a way of life from a very young age. When you own your own business and your food, clothing, and shelter, rely on that business, it is 24/7.

Not surprisingly, I suppose, when I left my parents' employ and ventured into the world of Corporate America, I retained that personal ownership of my work and my responsibilities. While I received glowing performance reviews, I was consistently reprimanded for not having enough work-life balance. To me, it was normal to work a lot and I liked it that way!

Which brings me to probably my biggest professional nemesis, whom I will call Katie. Katie was a walking excuse. In months of working with her, there was not one meeting where she was there on time. Her deliverables were always delayed, and her work was shoddy. Katie was my peer, we were both project managers within a pretty large PMO. I was not only appalled by her behavior and her river of excuses, I was dumbfounded that our manager did not seem to see the problem.

Katie's biggest excuse was that she was a single mother to a son. As a single mother to three daughters myself, that did not quite work for me. During a particularly stressful situation with my stakeholders, I realized that in order to deliver the quality expected, I would need to completely re-do the report that Katie had submitted. I stayed late at the office that night, re-working the report, validating the numbers, and ensuring it was accurate. The next morning as we sat down to review the report with the sponsor, Katie came in huffing and puffing, 10 minutes late.

As I looked at her with daggers, Katie began her stream of excuses:

"Jimmy did not want to get out of bed this morning and then I realized that his favorite shirt wasn't put in the dryer and he wanted eggs and bacon. It is so hard being a single...."

And just like that, I lost it. Epic meltdown. After being sequestered to my boss' office and given some time to cool down, he asked "why do you take her actions so personally?"

A scene from an Erin Brockovich played in my mind. Erin is sick but realizes that she is needed at the office. When she comes in, she learns that her boss has brought in representatives from another law office to assist. Her boss, Ed Massry, tells her that it's "not personal, Erin".

"Not personal? That is my WORK, my SWEAT, and my TIME AWAY FROM MY KIDS! If that is not personal, I don't know what is!" she responded.

Hell yes, it was personal. It was very personal. But should it have been? Maybe. Was my outburst appropriate? Absolutely not. This was probably the most pivotal event of my entire career. The meltdown to end all meltdowns earned me a ticket to a two-week intensive emotional intelligence program. Those two weeks were followed by an additional two weeks a month later. Four weeks. Four weeks away from job, my responsibilities, to figure myself out.

At first, I resisted the offer. But my boss made it clear that it was either that or I join the ranks of the unemployed. In my mind, I was a stellar employee. And I even falsely believed that they could not live without me. Guess what? The world goes on. Business goes on. Everyone is replaceable. So off I went to emotional intelligence training.

Looking back at that situation, and that infamous, very public meltdown, I realize it was the best possible thing that could happen to me. I needed to be slapped into reality and recognize that everything was not about me. Could I still find her behavior unacceptable? Of course! But could I control my emotions, my behaviors, and my response to her? Most definitely. And the key is emotional intelligence.

## Emotional Intelligence

The human body is a miraculous creation and we have barely begun to understand all the capabilities of the brain. Yet, we do know that there are three centers that influence our behavior. To understand emotional intelligence, we first need to understand those centers.

The brainstem, or our reptilian brain, is responsible for our involuntary functions, such as blood circulation, and govern our automatic instincts, such as fight or flight.

Beneath the neocortex and wrapping around the brainstem is the limbic area of the brain. Our emotions originate here. The limbic area, sometimes called the mammalian brain, stores our emotionally linked memories.

The neocortex is the part of our brain that controls rational thinking, including the higher brain functions of awareness; reason; voluntary movement; conscious, intentional thought; and language skills. We call this part of the brain the human brain.

While we would love to think our neocortex is in control of our emotions, oftentimes it is not:

You are happily driving down the road, listening to your favorite song, enjoying a beautiful day. Everything is rainbows and sunshine. Suddenly, some jerk (the bad guy) cuts you off, causing you to slam on your brakes to avoid hitting him. Your beautiful day, along with your sunny disposition, disappear.

You are furious and after laying on the horn for an extended period of time, you make a hand gesture and spew some colorful language at the perpetrator. Your heart rate and breathing have accelerated. Your pupils are dilated. Your blood flow is being redirected to your large muscles and you receive a big hit of adrenaline.

In less than a second, your brain reacted to a stimulus before the message even was able to reach your "human brain". Depending on the "bad guy's" emotional state, reactions, and awareness, he may respond back to you in a similar matter. In this situation, your brain is fighting with itself.

"There's a threat! I need to protect myself" screams the brainstem and limbic system.

"This is silly. No one got hurt. This could lead to a lot of trouble. I need to just back off." responds the neocortex.

Which one wins?

That really comes down to your understanding and mastery of emotional intelligence. It is important to recognize that the first reaction does not have to be maintained, nor do you need to beat yourself up for the knee-jerk reaction. It is all in how you handle the situation from that point forward. Knowing yourself and knowing your triggers are the best ways to prevent escalation.

According to Daniel Goleman's Mixed Model, there are five key attributes of emotional intelligence:

1. Self-awareness – the ability to know one's emotions, strengths, weaknesses, drives, values, and goals and recognize their impact on others while using gut feelings to guide decisions.
2. Self-regulation – controlling or redirecting one's disruptive emotions and impulses and adapting to changing circumstances.
3. Social skill – managing relationships to move people in the desired direction
4. Empathy – considering other people's feelings especially when making decisions
5. Motivation – being driven to achieve for the sake of achievement

Understanding and truly embracing emotional intelligence has allowed me to grow, mature, and perform at a higher capacity in project management, business management, and all aspects of leadership. I always highly recommend that project managers invest in emotional intelligence training, if it's possible.

## 9 – 9 – 9

For me, and many others that struggle with controlling our emotions, it is because we have a hard time putting the current situation into the proper perspective. The 9-9-9 model is a tool to assist you in developing perspective on situations, allowing you to take control of emotional or difficult situations.

When a situation escalates, and you are finding that you are justifying your emotional reaction to that situation, ask yourself these questions:

- Will this matter in 9 days?
- Will this matter in 9 months?
- Will this matter in 9 years?

I find that there are very few situations that will matter in nine months, let alone nine years. This is also a great technique to share with kids and teenagers who are going through some difficult or challenging situations.

## Pick the Messy Project

*"The best project is the hardest project I ever worked on. It had a very rigid timeline based on regulations and the project seemed almost impossible. The business put all other projects to the side for 12 months for us to succeed on this project. The project was a success in that we made it through, on time, on budget, within scope. The week before we closed on the project, an update came out on the regulation that excluded us from needing the project but in the end, we still*

*felt the project was in the best interest of our customers. It was an amazing time." Christine*

On the paradigm of risk comfort, where do you fall? Are you risk averse, seeking the safe way, repeatable processes, and work that falls within your comfort zone. Or do you live on the edge and step outside of that safe zone? As we gain more experience in our careers (AKA get older!), we tend to shy away from uncertainty and favor situations that are predictable and that we can easily control. And that may be acceptable if you are at the end of your career, just counting down the days until retirement or until you leave the company. But if you want to grow and reach new heights, it is time to step away from the comfort zone.

It is recognized that growth occurs in uncomfortable situations. Giving yourself an opportunity to challenge yourself, to grow and learn something new, to achieve something difficult, is a pathway to increased self-confidence and job satisfaction. While it can seem intimidating, stepping outside your comfort zone periodically is worth it.

Next time you are presented with a new, challenging and intimidating project, TAKE IT!

# Chapter 7 Action Plan

My key takeaways and "Ah-has!" from this chapter:

_____

_____

_____

Why these takeaways are important:

_____

_____

_____

Target dates for implementation:

_____

_____

_____

# Chapter 8

# Break the Cycle of Insanity

"Repeat the same action and expect a different outcome". Everyone recognizes this as the tongue-in-cheek definition of insanity. I have had the great experience of consulting with multiple companies across all industries as it relates to their project management. One of my biggest take-aways is that most of them are 'insane'!

Their projects fail repeatedly, yet they keep doing the same thing. Maybe they change the window dressing a bit: add a new process, implement a new procedure, develop a template. But they do not get to the root of what is causing the failure. It's rather like taking Tylenol for a headache that is being caused by a brain tumor.

## Learn From the Past

As with anything in life, our richest source of data is our past experiences. When we turn a blind-eye to the past, we fail to reap the benefit of our lessons learned. This is especially true in project management. There are so many lessons to be gained, not only from your individual experience, but also from the collective experiences of other people.

As a general rule of thumb, people do not like being wrong. This becomes even more of an issue as we age. If you notice, kids make mistakes all the time and are able to shrug it off. They do not get depressed, sullen, or discouraged. They brush it off and try again. They recognize, as do we, that it is through our mistakes that we grow and learn.

Yet, we do not have that same tolerance for ourselves and sometimes for other adults. No one is perfect. No project is perfect. Embrace your missteps and failures as a rich source of learning.

I love the Food Network on cable television. Watching the cooking shows, I became inspired to open a restaurant. The original thought was a small-town café type of establishment, however, our community happened to have a very large empty restaurant building just begging to be re-opened. Now, of course, it was empty because the two previous restaurants in that space failed (as do many restaurants). Always up for a challenge, I leased the space and threw everything I had physically, emotionally, and financially, into opening a beloved community restaurant, bar, and ice cream parlor.

(I bet you know where I am going with this story, right?)

I gave myself a three-month timeline to demo the interior, re-build, hire my staff, create my menu, and handle all the legal aspects of opening the restaurant. When the county health inspector visited he was incredibly impressed with the progress I was making and commented that he had never seen a project so well-run.

"Well, that is because I am a project manager first, restaurant owner second" I offered.

I'll skip to the end of this predictable story to save you all of the boring details. After six months of operations, the restaurant failed miserably. Despite fantastic project management (patting myself on the back), a great menu, fun and energized staff, ultimately there was not nearly enough

99

business to support the large overhead cost of keeping the restaurant going.

Was this failure painful? More than I could ever put into words. Would I do it again? Honestly, probably not! Was it valuable? Absolutely! There were so many things I learned, and I gained from the experience that could have only been taught through such a challenging scenario. My pride was bruised, my ego battered, but I came out of it much stronger. And this is the attitude we all need to have. Always ask yourself this question:

"What did I learn and what are my key takeaways?"

## The Beauty of Retrospectives

Agile project management appears to have taken the project management world by storm all of a sudden. In actuality, agile approaches have been around for quite a while, primarily used in software development projects. Recently the Project Management Institute (PMI) jumped on the bandwagon and began offering the PMI Agile Certified Practitioner (PMI-ACP)® credential and I started seeing agile practiced in many different environments.

There is a reason for the hype around agile – it works! A big caveat on that statement, of course, is that in order for it to be successful, the circumstance, the environment, and the people need to appropriate for an agile approach. Even if you do not use agile, there are some nuggets of awesomeness that can be pulled out and applied in any project situation. The most compelling of these is the use of retrospectives.

Agile teams use retrospectives frequently, on a set basis, and it allows for the team to have open and honest communication while also allowing for adjustments and tweaks to ensure that the team is maximizing their productivity. In a retrospective, we ask the following questions:

- What went well during this time period?
- What would we like to change for the next time period?
- How can we implement that change?

This immediate discussion, review, and action process allows the team to address any concerns or deficiencies while also acknowledging the wins. Having an open dialogue and discussion is akin to setting ground rules as we are able to really understand our teammates and how our project is progressing.

In agile project management, the work of the project is typically divided into sprints of one to four weeks and a sprint retrospective is performed after each sprint. In traditional or waterfall project management, I implement these retrospectives about every two weeks. I find that if it goes beyond two weeks, we tend to settle into work patterns or habits that can be harmful or detrimental to the project. By shaking things up every two weeks, I keep our productivity top-of-mind and allow for those adjustments to occur.

I recommend also incorporating a structured capture of lessons learned into the retrospectives. The process of documenting the lessons learned legitimizes the adjustments and creates a record or archive that can be applied on future projects. One of my biggest pet peeves is when organizations expect project managers to capture lessons learned at the end of the project, versus ongoing throughout the project.

Let's call a spade a spade, here. At the end of your project, no one cares anymore! They are moving on to their next project or their next task. Our memories become very selective and we lose a richness in our data when we wait until the end of our project. Capturing lessons learned at the end of the project is merely a check-the-box kind of task. To truly be impactful, lessons learned need to be captured and acted on throughout the project.

To facilitate the ongoing capture of lessons learned, I hand out notebooks to my team members. I want the notebook to be top-of-mind and to stand out, so I will typically go with something foolish like a "Hello Kitty" or "Trolls" notebook. I want it to be something that my team members cannot easily lose sight of in the midst of their workload. I nudge them frequently to be updating their notebooks and open up the discussion in team meetings for someone to share any lessons learned from that week. At the end of the project, I collect the notebooks and create a solid lessons learned report along with recommendations for improvement on future projects.

## Post-implementation Reports / Surveys

One of the most difficult things for us to do as emotional human beings is to place ourselves into a vulnerable position. Exposing ourselves to critique and feedback from others can be hurtful and embarrassing. This is even more poignant if we are already struggling with self-esteem issues, imposter syndrome, or other doubts. However, collecting feedback from your team members and stakeholders and developing a final post-implementation report should not be considered optional. Your perspective on these post-implementation reviews needs to be one of growth and improvement. Another example of needing high emotional intelligence!

While I recognized the importance of post-implementation reviews, I struggled with following through and executing them. While I was skeptical that the information was going to be leveraged, I also admit that the main reason was that I was hesitant to be so vulnerable. But one particular project that I was on changed all of that for me. I was able to see exactly how powerful the post-implementation review and survey were to improvement, both personally and organizationally.

Remember I mentioned that project in India? I was the project manager over the training aspect of the project, and Betsy was the overall project manager. Betsy had achieved her Project Management Professional (PMP)® and had led many successful initiatives for the organization. She was considered a high-caliber and driven project manager and was well-respected.

As my training team and I prepared to leave the United States and head to India, Betsy had given us very strict and somewhat meager budget allocations for our meals. The project manager in me applauded her structure, honesty, and forthright control of the project expenses. However, some team members felt that the budget for meals too small and they felt micromanaged by Betsy. All of the team members had tenure with the company, were mature and responsible, and were making a pretty significant personal sacrifice by leaving their homes for more than three weeks to execute the work of the project.

While we absolutely loved the country and loved our partners in India, extended days, long nights, and less-than-optimal working conditions had all of us looking forward to returning home after a few weeks. However, when an unforeseen technical glitch halted our training program, we realized we would need to stay an additional two weeks in order to complete all of the work. As a committed team, not one of us hesitated to stay and fulfill our commitments.

Upon completion of the project, Betsy sent out a survey to all the team members and another survey to stakeholders. I encouraged my team to provide honest and productive feedback in order to best enable Betsy, who was already a fantastic project manager, to improve further. After consolidating all of the survey results and analyzing the results, Betsy called the leadership team in for a review meeting. At that time, I had been with the organization for a few years and it was the first time I had seen someone do this.

The project certainly had not been easy. It was the first of its kind for the organization and the technical issue caused the project to come in over budget and slightly behind schedule. However, Betsy bravely faced all of the feedback and provided honest reflection on the results of the project. She recognized that her extreme focus on costs alienated some of the team members who were certainly going above-and-beyond to make the project a success. Betsy learned from the experience and emerged even stronger!

# Chapter 8 Action Plan

My key takeaways and "Ah-has!" from this chapter:

_____

_____

_____

Why these takeaways are important:

_____

_____

_____

Target dates for implementation:

_____

_____

_____

# Chapter 9

# Be a Perpetual Learner

I believe that professional project managers are on a path to business leadership and strategic roles. Gone are the days when a project manager was simply considered a task manager or a glorified babysitter to a bunch of overgrown man- and woman-babies. While there are certainly still organizations out there with that mentality, they are rapidly becoming the exception versus the rule. So consider this your pep-talk and your slap on the behind to "go out there and get 'em!'".

While the *PMBOK® Guide* is incredibly stimulating (note my sarcasm here), there are also a lot of other resources and techniques for growing and learning. In Shawshank Redemption, Red exclaims "Get busy living or get busy dying!". I apply that to project management: get busy learning or get busy retiring. As project managers, we cannot afford to slack off, back off, or slide into contentment and confidence based on our subject matter expertise. We must make a commitment to growing and learning and expanding our skill sets.

## The Project Management Institute (PMI)

If you are a project manager, you need to get plugged in to PMI. The benefits of PMI membership are significant. You receive discounts on credentials, have electronic access to practice standards and member-only content at no cost on PMI.org, and you will receive the PM Network® magazine as well as the quarterly research journal. Annual PMI membership costs are on-par with similar organizations:

- Individual membership: $129 to join plus a $10 application fee and $129 to renew

- Student membership: $32 to join and $32 to renew
- Retiree membership: $65 to renew (after at least five years of active membership)

As of the publication of this book, PMI offers eight certifications:

- Project Management Professional (PMP)®
- Certified Associate in Project Management (CAPM)®
- Program Management Professional (PgMP)®
- PMI Schedule Management Professional (PMI-SP)®
- PMI Risk Management Professional (PMI-RMP)®
- PMI Agile Certified Practitioner (PMI-ACP)®
- Portfolio Management Professional (PfMP)®
- PMI Professional in Business Analysis (PMI-PBA)®

## Project Management Certification

Many professional project managers seek out certification and the premier certification is the Project Management Professional (PMP)® designation. Certainly not for the faint of heart, the PMP is a globally recognized credential that is earned upon submitting enough hours and years of experience as well as passing a very challenging 200-

question exam. Of the certifications available in the market, the PMP is the PiMP-daddy (see what I did there?).

Created and administered by PMI®, the first PMP certification exam was held on 6 October 1984 and of the 56 individuals that participated, 43 passed. As of October 31, 2017, there are more than 794,000 PMP credential holders globally. The PMP credential recognizes professional project managers with demonstrated experience and knowledge of leading and directing project management teams.

## PMP Requirements

To qualify to apply for the PMP credential, you must meet the following criteria:

With a high school diploma or global equivalent:

- Minimum of five years / 60 months non-overlapping professional project management experience with at least 7,500 hours leading and directing the project within the last eight consecutive years *and*

- 35 contact hours of formal education in project management

With a bachelor's degree or global equivalent:

- Minimum of three years / 36 months non-overlapping professional project management experience with at least 7,500 hours leading and directing the project within the last eight consecutive years *and*

- 35 contact hours of formal education in project management

For more information on pursuing your PMP, check out our site for up-to-date credential and application information:

https://www.pmlearningsolutions.com/pmp-credential-overview

## CAPM Requirements

For those project managers that do not have enough project management experience to pursue the PMP credential, PMI also offers the Certified Associate in Project Management (CAPM)®. The CAPM is a fantastic certificate for those who are newer to project management or maybe have had a lapse in their experience. The CAPM certification is valid for a period of five years. At that point, the candidate could choose to either re-take the CAPM exam or, if enough experience has been gained, pursue PMP certification. The CAPM is 150-questions and tests candidates over the

*PMBOK® Guide.* Information on the CAPM certification can be found on our site:

https://www.pmlearningsolutions.com/capm-certification-overview

As a holder of six of the certifications, needless to say I believe in the value of certifications and credentials. While multi-year degrees are still a standard employment requirement for management roles, I am finding a significant increase in the number of organizations and industries seeking project managers with their PMP certification; in some instances, valuing the PMP higher than a degree. This is due in part to the fact that in order to earn the PMP you must have significant project management experience.

(Steps on to soapbox)

Just because someone has a PMP certification, it does not guarantee that they are a good project manager or an effective project manager. It does not even mean that their projects were successful or that they are liked and respected within their organization. It simply shows that the project manager had the necessary experience, had the drive to seek certification, and was able to pass an exam. A very difficult exam.

As difficult as the exam can be, it does not necessarily reflect the skills needed for real-world project management. Because project management is not a one-size-fits-all job or role, it would be impossible to test candidates on the practical application of various project management approaches. Other than the PgMP, none of the credentials are based on any type of feedback from peers, clients, supervisors, or team members.

I feel the need to write this as I have encountered people who feel that if you are a good project manager, you can pass the PMP exam. And if you do not have your PMP, you must not be a good project manager.

On the other hand, I have also encountered plenty of people who feel that certification is a waste of time and indicates absolutely nothing about capability. Some people resist certification to the point that they believe that anyone who happens to have one must not be a good project manager.

In my experience, working with hundreds of project managers, I can attest to the fact that there are excellent project managers that are certified. There are excellent project managers that are not certified. There are horrible project managers that are certified. There are horrible project managers that are not certified.

I always find it a bit humorous how bitter people become about the credential if they have failed the PMP exam. I teach PMP exam preparation and I vividly remember a vitriolic conversation with a past student.

He called me to inform how the PMP was a bunch of "crap" (not what he really said) and that I was a horrible excuse for a project manager. He went on to say that I cannot possibly even know how to manage a real project given that I have six PMI certifications. "Go back to your ivory tower, lock the door, and throw away the key". Yes, that is an exact quote from him. And yes, I'm still looking for my ivory tower.

So based on all of that, do I recommend getting certified? You bet! It simply provides a source of legitimization to your field and to your experience (again with the big asterisk that a PMP does not make you a magical, all-powerful, immune-to-failure, superhero!). But if you can get it, I certainly would.

## Keep Learning

There are multiple ways to keep your skills up and learn about new trends in the industry, find best practices, and mature your project management capabilities and strengths.

There are PMI Chapters located all over the globe. Find your local chapter and get plugged in. Keep in mind that chapters are volunteer run and can always use more volunteers. Most chapters offer learning sessions typically once per month. The chapter will host a speaker on a relevant project management topic and participants earn professional development units (PDUs) or continuing education credits for attending. This is fantastic for those individuals with their PMP or other PMI certifications.

Another great way to grow and learn is by developing a self-organized project management center of excellence. Find other engaged and interested project managers and collaborate on improving skills, processes, and results.

And last, but certainly not least, READ! PM Network articles, books on project management, books on leadership, blogs. There is so much great information out there – go get it!

# Chapter 9 Action Plan

My key takeaways and "Ah-has!" from this chapter:

_____

_____

_____

Why these takeaways are important:

_____

_____

_____

Target dates for implementation:

_____

_____

_____

# Afterword

If it is not evident throughout this book, I am incredibly passionate about project management. I fully believe that in this day and age, companies have no choice but to grow, change, and update in order to be competitive and successful. That change must be managed well and that is where project management comes in to play. Without effective project management, companies will not be sustainable.

When I work with organizations on their project management maturity, I use my model of project management excellence to not only evaluate their current maturity, but also to identify their opportunities for growth.

The five elements to The Goodrich Model of Project Management Excellence are symbiotic in nature, but the foundation must be the purpose and exceptional growth is a result of passion. Between the purpose and the passion is the organization's product, people, and process.

The first thing to evaluate is the **PURPOSE** of the organization and the work of the organization.

THE
GOODRICH MODEL

PASSION

PEOPLE

PROCESS

PRODUCT

PURPOSE

**PROJECT MANAGEMENT EXCELLENCE®**

- Does the organization have a clear strategic direction?

- What is the culture of the organization? (growth, innovative, hierarchical, patriarchal, commodity, familial, etc?)

- Is the vision, mission, and strategic direction communicated and understood through all levels of the organization?

The middle trio of **PEOPLE, PRODUCT,** and **PROCESS** are the core of project management excellence.

In considering the **PEOPLE** involved in project management, I ask the following questions:

- Are the employees that are involved in project management actively engaged in growing the business?

- Do they have adequate growth and project management skill development opportunities?

120

- How is morale, conflict management, and attrition within the project management teams and organizations?

- What is the average tenure of the project managers and project resources?

- What percentage of employees are contract versus full-time within the project environment?

In considering the **PRODUCTS** produced by the project management teams, I ask the following questions:

- What is the primary business line of the organization? Are there any current or potential complimentary business lines?

- What percentage of project management effort is spent on managing existing products versus adding new products?

- Who are the primary competitors and what is your organization's product differentiator?

In considering the **PROCESSES** used by the project management teams, I ask the following questions:

- What is the project management maturity of the organization? Of the project managers?

- Is there a method to capture and distribute lessons learned?

- What is the rigidity versus flexibility of the processes involved in project management?

- Do people have clearly defined project management roles?

- Is there a consistent approach, methodology, and utilization of project management templates?

Lastly, I always want to validate the **PASSION** of the employees and the organization as it relates to growth, change, and achievement.

- What is the primary passion of the organization?
- Is it top-down, bottom-up, or randomly encountered?
- Is your passion evident to your clients and customers? Your employees? Your community?
- How well does the passion permeate the organization and all activities within the organization?

Evaluating and understanding these five aspects of project management allow for the discovery of potential improvements, growth, and challenges.

Interested in learning more about the model or learning how I can assist your organization? Send me a message! https://www.belindagoodrich.com/#contact

# About the Author

Globally recognized as a project management expert, Belinda Goodrich is the founder and CEO of The Goodrich Institute and PM Learning Solutions. PM Learning Solutions, formerly known as Passionate Project Management, is focused on delivering world-class project management exam preparation programs and materials. Under The Goodrich Institute, Belinda serves as a consultant to a number of Fortune 500 companies with a focus on improving the project management processes and practices in order to drive business growth.

After over 20 years of corporate project management and executive leadership experience, Belinda "retired" to serve the project management community. The first woman in the world to achieve five of the PMI credentials, Belinda now holds the following: PMP®, CAPM®, PMI-SP®, PMI-ACP®, PMI-RMP®, PgMP®. In addition, Belinda is a Certified Scrum Master. With a focus on industrial and organizational psychology, Belinda is fascinated with the mind, emotions, and behaviors of project managers and stakeholders and she leverages that fascination to bring practical application to project management techniques.

The author of multiple books and courseware on project management and PMI exam topics, Belinda is an in-demand facilitator, speaker, and consultant. As an instructor, Belinda has helped thousands of project managers achieve their project management credentials. Her passion is creating the connection between theoretical project management concepts and real-world business needs through energetic and engaging sessions.

In 2018, Belinda will be releasing a co-authored book *The Will to Win* with famed leadership experts Jim Cathcart and Brian Tracy. In addition, her soon-to-be released book *SHIFT: Business Growth through Exceptional Project Management* is already garnering positive attention from industry leaders.

**Facebook:** www.facebook.com/PMBelindaSpeaks/
**Twitter:** @TheBeGoodrich
**Linkedin:** www.linkedin.com/in/belindagoodrich/
www.PMLearningSolutions.com
www.BelindaGoodrich.com

Made in the USA
Middletown, DE
21 September 2019